This book belongs to:

Color With Me!

Cousin & Me Christmas Adventures!

Sandy Mahony
Mary Lou Brown

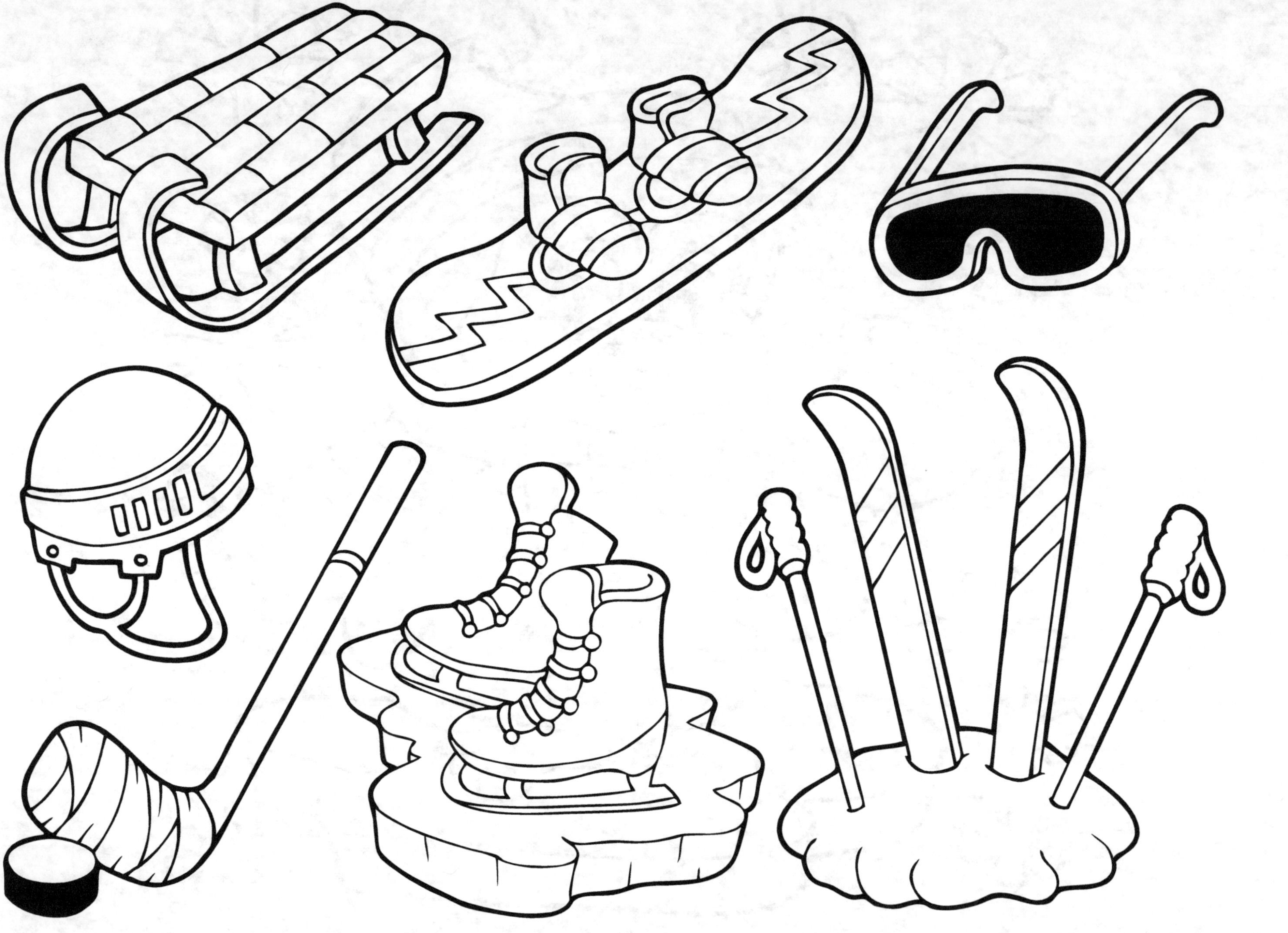

adventurelearningpress.com

www.ingramcontent.com/pod-product-compliance
Lightning Source LLC
Chambersburg PA
CBHW081805280526
45789CB00008B/3001
9781540523570